Betty Bee - Rhyme With Me

Author Marissa Phifer

Illustrations by
Eminence Systems

THIS BOOK BELONGS TO:

_____

Published by:

www.marissaphifer.com

Copyright © 2021 Marissa Phifer

All rights reserved.

ISBN: 978-1-7368124-1-9

This book is dedicated to my parents and bonus parents,
James & Margaret, Joseph & Karen;
To all the young children reading this book;
And to my support system! You know who you are!

Phil 4:13

I love to rhyme so joyfully.

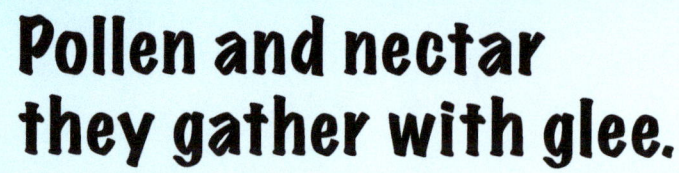

Pollen and nectar they gather with glee.

But they will need more help, you see!

the help needed for this collecting spree!

Look at the bees near Bee Keeper Magee.

They are neighbors from the next colony!

I shout out loud, and make a plea.

"Please help my friends, Bees One, Two, and Three."

"Please grab a bag and follow me"—

"to flowers big and tall, you see!"

"Bags filled to the brim, we shout, yippie!"

to find my friends and for rhyming with me.

BETTY BEES – RHYMING WORDS

Bee Joyfully Key Me

Tree Bumblebees Three Sea

Harmony Jubilee Foresee Spree

Flee Colony Plea Yippie

Agree Free Guarantee

www.ingramcontent.com/pod-product-compliance
Lightning Source LLC
Chambersburg PA
CBHW041707160426

43209CB00017B/1768